MW00697382

TELL YOUR SECRET

A companion to the book:
Break Free From Your Dirty Little Secrets:
A New You in 10 Secret-Breaking Stages

GRETCHEN HYDO

Tell Your Secret

Gretchen Hydo

Los Angeles, CA

Coach@GretchenHydo.com

Ordering Information:

Special discounts are available on quantity purchases by corporations, associations, educational institutions, and others. For details, contact Gretchen Hydo above.

Printed in the United States of America

First Edition

Hardcover ISBN 978-1-5136-9936-3

Publisher

Winsome Entertainment Group LLC

Sandy, UT

Inside you'll discover:

STAGE ONE:
CALLING OUT YOUR SECRET
· BREAKING THE RULES
· SHEDDING YOUR SECRETS

STAGE TWO:
UNWIRING YOUR SECRET
· DEFINE YOUR FAULTY WIRING
· DEFINING YOUR TRIPWIRE
· BUCKING YOUR BELIEFS
· FORGING NEW PATTERNS AND BELIEFS

STAGE THREE:
CHASING THE ROOT FEELINGS
· DEFINING YOUR ROOT FEELING
· COST AND PAYOFF

STAGE FOUR:
FACING YOUR FALSE SELF
· LIVING IN SHADOW BEHAVIOR
· DEFINING YOUR PATTERNS
· PUTTING IT TOGETHER
· WHAT DID YOU WANT TO BE AS A KID?
· SEEING CLEARLY

STAGE FIVE:
BUILDING YOUR FAITH
· UNDERSTANDING YOUR FOUNDATION
· COLLECTING EVIDENCE
· CLUES TO YOUR TRUE SELF

STAGE SIX:
PREPARING TO TELL YOUR SECRET
· SECRETS AND SICKNESS
· FACING YOUR PSYCHOLOGICAL CONTRACTS
· TAKING A RISK ASSESSMENT

STAGE SEVEN:
TELL YOUR SECRET
· IDENTIFYING WHO TO TELL CHECKLIST
· SURRENDER YOUR SECRET

STAGE EIGHT:
STOP CREATING SECRETS
· DEFINING YOUR LIMITING BELIEFS
· FORGIVENESS OF THE FALSE SELF
· DAILY SECRET-KEEPING CHECK IN

STAGE NINE:
DEATH OF THE OLD YOU
· KNOW YOUR TRIGGERS
· GETTING TO KNOW YOU
· DEFINE YOUR HIGHEST VALUES
· CREATE YOUR "I WON'T LIST"
· NOTICE WHAT OTHERS NOTICE ABOUT YOU

STAGE TEN:
CREATING YOUR RIPPLE EFFECT
· NOTICING YOUR RIPPLE
· FINDING YOUR OXYGEN MASK
· A LIFE OF ACTION

Lovely woman–

I know we haven't met. I don't know you; you don't know me. But I do know the human heart. I know about keeping secrets and the shame they cause. I know about hiding behind them, bending the truth and wanting to be free from my false, smaller self, who is afraid. I know about wanting to feel different, what it's like for my skin to not fit right, and being sick in my head and sick in my body. I know about acting out, being too loud and being too small. I know about keeping secrets to look good and to fit in. And I know about the versions of myself that I've created to feel safe, loved, and valued. Maybe you know something about this too?

Every single one of us has a secret that we're hiding. And even though you might think your secret is unique, it's not. We all have a story to tell, internal rules to break, and a big life to live! As you embark on your secret-shredding, rule-busting journey, know that I'm here with you. I've done the work, cried the tears, and walked the thousand-mile journey to the other side to set things right. I'm holding out my hand to you to pull you forward because the truth is, it's time to let your false self go. It's time to forgive her for what she didn't know and let her step into the new bigger and better container of life that she is meant for. That should make you excited (and maybe a little bit terrified).

This companion workbook, to my book, Break Free from Your Dirty Little Secrets: A New You in 10 Secret-Breaking Stages, is a side-by-side guide to help women break free from the shame they've been holding because of their secrets. It is a tool to give voice to the truth. It is a gong of encouragement to end the cycle of secret keeping, outdated mindsets, and playing by everyone else's rules.

It's time to let the cat out of the bag, ladies. It's time to tell your secret!

Much love, Gretchen

Stage ONE

CALLING OUT YOUR SECRET

Today is the day that you will start to break free from your dirty little secrets, the shame that's holding you back, and your false identity.

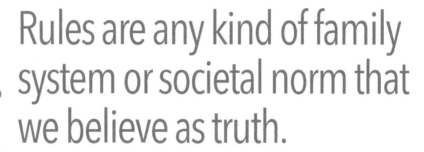

Rules are any kind of family system or societal norm that we believe as truth.

They are often generational or institutional and we must question if they work for us, or we begin telling lies, hiding who we truly are, and living in the shadows of life.

Rules are important because they shape the way we live our lives AND they have the ability to make us secret keepers, causing us to dwell in the shadows of small living.

Rules can be all sorts of things that we pick up as ways to be, truths to hold, and behaviors that we think we are supposed to subscribe to.

The problem is that these rules have been given to us from someone else; we haven't chosen them for ourselves. Here are some examples of rules put on others by society and well-meaning loved ones:

Women should always have long hair and carry a nice purse. (What if you like short hair and carry a backpack?)

Polite women don't speak up. (Great way to become a people pleaser or to be seen as a b*tch if you do.)

Good mothers stay home with their kids. (Way to feel bad if you love your job or have to work.)

Pretty women are a size 4 or smaller. (Nice way to create body dysmorphia, anorexia, bulimia and low self-esteem.)

It's unsafe to travel alone as a woman. (Really? So we should stay at home and wait around for someone to go with us and put our lives on hold?)

...and on and on and on.

Write down as many rules as you can think of that were a part of your family's conditioning and social system.

What ideas or actions do you avoid because they would upset someone else?

Hint: Think about all of the places you tell yourself you "should" fill in the blank. If there is a should, there is a rule linked to it.

Hint: Anytime you are worried about people pleasing someone else, you are following an internal rule. Let's find it.

Write down the ways you break these rules,
even though you know they are a part of your
rule book.

Which actions or thoughts become secrets?

Hint: Anything you don't want someone to know about is a secret.

Which of your rules have you
adopted but don't want to follow?

Secrets deliver a one-two-three punch. The first swing is the secret action, which becomes "the secret"; the second jab is the false story that you now tell yourself

about who you are because of the secret action and the secret (e.g., I am the worst kind of worst because I had an affair and, therefore, am inherently untrustworthy for life), and the knock-out punch is the why behind the secret action–ultimately the " big secret" (e.g., childhood conditioning and faulty wiring taught you low self-esteem and the belief there isn't enough love to go around for you). It's exhausting living life in the boxing ring.

Today is the day that you will start to break free from your dirty little secrets, the shame that's holding you back, and your false identity. As you work through this journal, choose one secret to take through all ten stages. Once you have worked your first secret through the process, you can come back and use this on all of your secrets.

What is the one secret that you would like to become free from? Maybe it's the one you hate yourself for. Maybe it's the one that you still feel sick or numb over. Maybe those secrets are too big, and you need to start with a softer, gentler secret. No matter what secret you choose, commit to taking it through all ten stages because relief is on the other side of this process.

What is your secret action?

What is it? What did you do?

Once we take an action we're ashamed of and make it a secret, our critical narrator gets involved and creates a secret-story about who we are because of the action we took. This secret-story is always based on lack and deficiency. It tells us that we aren't good enough, not worth it, and keeps us in shame. The story also becomes the lens we see life through, which causes us to take on an identity that does not serve who we are.

What story does your critical narrator say about who you are because of this action?

Pause and apply empathy to your situation. As you take a deep breath and acknowledge your courage, know that you have taken the first step towards freedom.

Now that you've called out your secret, be kind to yourself. You may want to relax and take it easy, or you may want to go out and exercise and get it out of your body.

Journal your thoughts here

UNWIRING YOUR SECRET

We have to go back to the foundation of childhood to see how our wires got crossed in the first place and caused us to go to such great lengths to keep ourselves safe behind our long-embedded secrets.

What is faulty wiring anyway?

What is faulty wiring anyway? Think of it as a defective piece of your brain's communication system that picks up and morphs signals from the outside world. When a belief is created and becomes a mismanaged need, that is your new navigation tool for survival. Life is run by a false self. When you look at the faulty messages that you believe about yourself and the world, you will begin to unravel the reasons why you create and keep secrets. Faulty wiring isn't good or bad; it just doesn't belong to your true self. In your false self, it's created a reality that you believe is true and live up to. At its core, faulty wiring becomes the navigation tool you use to problem solve and chart your course in life.

As you unwire your faulty wiring, think of the childhood stories and situations that have shaped you, and your behaviors that have been created as tools for survival. These tools often become the three of the one-two-three secret-keeping punch.

What events occurred in your life that caused faulty wiring/messages?

What family system did you learn and use to navigate the world?

What do you believe about yourself or the world because of these navigation tools?

How did your faulty wiring contribute to your secret that you are taking through the 10-stage Secret-Breaking System?

Once you have an idea of your faulty wiring, you begin to embark on one of the most important reasons that you create secrets: your tripwires.

A tripwire is a deep, long embedded feeling or emotion that is rooted in the past and caused by the faulty wiring of your false self. It's one of the main reasons that you keep and create secrets. When tripped, this emotion causes us to take actions that in our truest and most healed self we would never take. Tripwire emotions run the gamut and can range from feeling: less than, disregarded, not enough, unworthy, forgotten, devalued, unloved, unwanted, abandoned, like a burden and more.

Go back to the secret that you're working through and answer the following questions:

What tripwire emotion was triggered to create this secret?

What action did you take because of your faulty wiring or tripwire?

List all of your tripwire emotions connected to your secret.

Hint: if you get hysterical over it, it's historical and probably your trigger point.

It's time to buck this belief system that has supported your faulty wiring!

A belief is something that we take as being true. We hold it as fact in our belief system (or as I like to call B.S.). Beliefs about who we are can cause substantial amounts of damage and lead to further secret-keeping.

Keep working through your secret as you answer the following questions:

What beliefs were you given by your parents and others that led to your secret? List as many as you can.

Circle the ones that aren't true for you and that you would like to let go of.

What is a more empowering
belief you can employ?

HINT: You don't have to believe it
today, you will adopt it over time.

As we continue to unravel your secret,

it's important to look at the beliefs that you've picked up along the way that may have contributed to secret-keeping.

Think about what you kept to yourself and hid from your parents about school, boys, your friends, sex, drinking, where you really were, who you were with in the car, what you really wore, where you got that lipstick, and whatever else you didn't want them to know. What responses did you have to telling the whole truth? Your reaction is part of your conditioning.

What were you conditioned to believe about sharing and asking about personal information with others?

What behavior was
rewarded in your family?

What beliefs are you willing
to let go of right now?

*Dirty Little
Deep Dives*

Exploring your faulty
wiring will help you
begin to unravel
your reasons for
keeping secrets.

Faulty wiring can be rewired.

As you make new choices,
your world will open up to
new paths of possibility.

When we listen for what we
need, we can answer with
our new beliefs.

CHASING THE ROOT FEELINGS

We will be exploring the root feelings you chased behind

your faulty wiring, and tripwire emotions brought on by

the action behind our big secret.

Consciously or unconsciously, you are always measuring where you fit based on your root feeling.

The root feelings that we chase, look for, and crave based on our faulty wiring often are connected to love—the first and most basic root feeling that everyone is after and has a right to have. Other root feelings are worthiness, security, belonging, safety, satisfaction, self-worth, freedom, and fun. Like a drug addict, we are willing to take almost any action to feel a root feeling. They are primal and we have been taught we need to take secret actions to get our needs met.

To keep unraveling your secret so that we can continue to find more of your true self, we need to explore the root feeling at the center.

What is the root feeling that you craved the most while creating that secret?

Examples: love, protection, belonging

When life is created from a critical narrative, instead of expanding, we retract. When we retract, we look for protection and lean on our secrets to keep us safe, thus creating a false version of who we are: our false self. In this false you, the beliefs you hold about yourself because of your secrets have taken root and sprouted. The more you believe the lies about you, the farther away you get from your true self.

What's the story your false self tells you about the root feeling?
Your faulty wiring may give you some clues.

Example: To be loved, I need to be protected.
If I am not being protected, I am not really being loved.

What faulty wiring moments are embedded in that need?

Think of your secret.
Write it here:

What is the payoff that you get from chasing your root feeling?

_____

What is the payoff that you get from keeping your secret safe?

What's it costing you to live this way?

As we continue

to Stage Four, *Facing Your False Self,* *it's time to put on your big girl panties. It's showdown time with your false self. We start to catch glimpses of the most authentic version of you, your true self. Your true self will make a powerful claim over your life from the shroud of secrets. That is the new payoff. As you begin to get to know your true self and trust her, you will take action on her behalf. Those actions might feel shaky at first and you may be uncertain as you take them. But do take them. As you do, your life will change by letting go of one secret at a time.*

I'm with you, *Gretchen*

Dirty Little Deep Dives

Identifying the root feeling of your secret will help you unravel your secret-keeping behavior.

If it's hysterical, it's historical.

Your secret's cost and payoff have cost you enough.

When your false self starts to take the lead, take a pause.

Stage FOUR

FACING YOUR
FALSE SELF

Good enough living is missing the <u>more</u> of your true self.

A shadow behavior is a behavior we take based on our false self.

When our beliefs and behaviors spin out of control because of our core secret created out of faulty wiring, life cannot offer us anything more than our own recycled thinking.

**Journal any thoughts you have about
Living in Shadow Behavior here.**

It's time to get the information about your one secret in front of you.

so that you can begin to uncover your secret creating pattern. Refer back to your answers in Chasing The Root Feeling in Stage Three.

What root feeling did you chase because of your secret?

What action did you take because of the root feeling?

What tripwire was set off in the creation of this secret?

What faulty wiring navigation tool did you use?

What story did you tell yourself about who you
are because of the action you took while
chasing a feeling?

What kind of good enough living
have you subscribed to because of
this pattern?

Take a moment and digest your pattern. You had a root feeling that you wanted. You took an action to get it. Your tripwire emotion set off your quest for your root feeling. You took a bigger action based on your faulty wiring's navigation system to get the root feeling...and boom, a secret was created.

What story did your false self tell you about the pattern and who you are because of the action you took?

> "
> To change, we first have to get serious about calling out our shadow behaviors that perpetuate our secret-keeping.
>
> *Gretchen*

Journal about it here:

Take your secret that you are running through the system and do the following:

From the list of shadow behaviors, check off any ways of being that you display in your false self. (Bookmark this page as you will need it for Part 5.)

☐ Procrastination and paralysis

☐ Overeating (eating all the donuts and saying they went bad)

☐ Lying and truth-bending

☐ Perfectionism

☐ Obsessing

☐ Violence

☐ Overly nice

☐ Flying off the handle

☐ Being over-emotional

☐ Detachment and lack of vulnerability

☐ Unable to follow through

☐ Checking up on others

☐ Bad relationships

☐ Promiscuity

☐ Addictions

☐ Self-sabotage

☐ Negative self-talk

☐ People pleasing

☐ Argumentative

☐ Intimidating

☐ Doormat

☐ Self-importance

☐ Overdoing/over committing

☐ Others:

_____

_____

_____

_____

How did the shadow behavior contribute to your secret action?

Write out how your shadow behavior is part of your false self's narrative.

STAGE FOUR

FACING YOUR FALSE SELF
PART 4: WHAT DID YOU WANT TO BE AS A KID?

As you answer the following questions, have fun and don't let your false self edit your responses

to make them sound smart or make sense.
Your little girl holds clues to your mission in life.

What did you want to be when you grew up? When
you were a kid? A teen? A young adult? Thirty?

What games did you used to play?

How did you imagine your future?

What parts of these answers still have energy around them today?

What small action can you take to usher in your younger self's knowing?

Did you feel it?

Did you feel that glimmer as you uncovered a piece of who you truly are? Run with it, ladies. Keep it close to you. Put an action around it.

XO, Gretchen

It's time to revisit your key shadow behaviors you checked in Part 3.

Copy them here.

What are your reasons for using these behaviors as a go-to?

What's the truth about who you really are?

How can you use this behavior differently?

The greatest obstacle that keeps us from moving forward is shame.

Dirty Little Deep Dives

Your younger self holds the clues to your purpose and mission.

Your true self can be trusted.

You can change your behavior at any time.

We all have a golden buddha inside of us.

BUILDING YOUR FAITH

A faith relationship is cooperative and becomes a

knowing between you and this greater intelligence.

To untwist shame, we need faith. Big faith.

This faith relationship will help us to go deeper than what's on the chaotic surface of the false self. A faith relationship is cooperative and becomes a knowing between you and this greater intelligence.

Who presented the first view for you of spirituality, God, and/or religion?

What was that view?

Did it leave a positive or negative effect on your life?

Positive   *Negative*

What moments in your life have marked and shaped your spiritual path?

_____

How do you believe that faith or spirituality has an impact on your life?

What are your current spiritual beliefs?

What kind of a relationship do you have with a God of your understanding?

What do you believe about that relationship and spiritual entity?

What do you do to connect to a power greater than yourself?

As you begin to build a new life, your true self will guide you.

But it's going to take faith. Faith in your true self and faith in a divine spiritual power who will help you to let go of your old ways of being, your patterns, and your secrets.

Where have you felt a power greater than yourself in your life?

What miracles have you encountered?

_____

What moments in your life can you catalog and ask yourself: was it odd or God?

As we get to know our true selves, clues to our mission in life emerge.

It's important to consider them, even if they feel big and overreaching.

What inklings do you have about your purpose that you would like
to explore, even if you aren't quite ready to pack your bags?

What have your "angels with skin on" encouraged you to do along your path?

Building a faith foundation

is a key to living a joyful life full of satisfaction and purpose, and as you evolve, so will your understanding and relationship with your God.

You don't have to get it all at once, in fact, you won't. **What's important is that you start.**

You got this, Gretchen

Dirty Little Deep Dives

Your faith will carry you through breaking your secrets.

Your God has always been with you.

God is personal and not one-size-fits-all.

God will help you with your dirty little secrets.

PREPARING TO TELL YOUR SECRET

Once you tell your secret, it is almost impossible to go backward

in your behavior because you have set a new standard that is so

full of integrity, it doesn't doesn't allow for backsliding

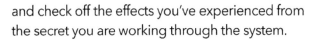

Take a moment

and check off the effects you've experienced from
the secret you are working through the system.

- ☐ Missing work

- ☐ Avoiding social situations

- ☐ Feeling anxious, depressed, sad, shameful, fearful

- ☐ Angry explosions

- ☐ Loss of sleep

- ☐ Addictive behaviors

- ☐ Loss of appetite

- ☐ Unexplained physical ailments (headaches, stomachs, ulcers, frequently not feeling well)

- ☐ Others:

_____

_____

_____

Time for a feeling check. How are you doing?

Every relationship you're a part of has a psychological contract associated with it.

These contracts are the unwritten expectations that each person agrees to, even if the agreement is never spoken. Answer these questions about your current psychological agreement attached to your one secret.

Who is the psychological contract with?

What is the contract/exchange?

I will get this and in exchange, you will get that.

How did this contract lead to
your secret?

How old were you when
you made the contract?

Age contract was initiated

How do you feel about the contract today?

What are you sad, angry, hurt, and scared of because of this contract?

What are you grateful for that this contract taught you?

How would you like to change this contract?

Would you like to cancel it? Make it null and void?
Or revise it? If so, how would you like to revise it?

Take these prompts and put them in letter form. Do not physically give the agreement to anyone. This is a step for you to process and to prepare so that you can begin to tell your secrets without being ensnared in the agreement.

As of today, I am changing the contract between me and _____.

The initial contract that _____

_____

_____

_____ is null and void.

The new agreement is _____

_____

_____

_____

_____.

_____
Signature

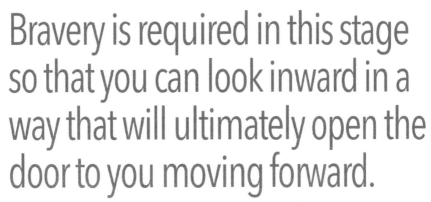

Bravery is required in this stage so that you can look inward in a way that will ultimately open the door to you moving forward.

Boldness, empathy, honesty, and goodwill toward self are a requirement for taking a thorough and compassionate inventory of your secret.

What is your biggest fear about telling your secret?

What is it costing you to keep your secret?

What will you miss out on if you continue to live the way you're living?

Are you protecting anyone with your secret?

You? Someone else? Name who.

What are you imagining would happen to them if you revealed the secret?

What are you imagining would happen to you if you told?

On a scale of 1–10 how likely is it that these imagined consequences will occur?

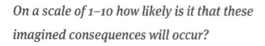

1   2   3   4   5   6   7   8   9   10

On a scale of 1–10 how likely is it that these imagined consequences will occur to you?

1   2   3   4   5   6   7   8   9   10

On a scale of 1–10 how likely is it that these imagined consequences will occur to them?

1   2   3   4   5   6   7   8   9   10

If these situations or scenarios did happen,
what would you do to take care of yourself?

Preparing to tell your secret: template

Run your secret through this template. You don't have to share it with anyone. The risks are so much lower than you think, and the benefits are so much higher than you can imagine.

Secret action	I had unprotected sex which led to me putting a baby up for adoption.
Critical narrative	I am irresponsible and unworthy of being a mother.
Big secret	I put the baby up for adoption because if I didn't my dad would disown me because I would be an embarrassment and unlovable.
Ailment	Mental illness anxiety/eating disorder
Who the psychological contract is with	My dad because he didn't ask, and I didn't tell (even though he knew).
Consequences	A child I gave up for adoption I have never seen.
Risk asessment	Shatters a wholesome image, endangers the relationship with dad, causes problems with parents and current husband and children.
Who I harmed	Myself, the baby

Secret action

Critical narrative

Big secret

Ailment

Who the psychological contract is with

Consequences

Risk assessment

Who I harmed

Let's put the brakes on

the actual telling of your secret until we get to Stage Seven where I lay out the process of how, when, and to whom you share your truth. Right now, at this moment, I want you to give a big HELL, YEAH to the emotional, physical, and psychological damage your secrets will no longer cause you. Girl, shake the false self off! Are you ready to take the next stage?

Let's go, *Gretchen*

Dirty Little Deep Dives

It's time to cancel your psychological agreements.

You can live a kick-ass life.

Letting go of good makes way for great.

Stage SEVEN

TELL YOUR SECRET

The point in sharing your secret is never to hurt someone else or yourself. It's to come clean about the secret you've been hiding and to reveal those truths so you can stop the patterns of the false self . . . and stop creating more secrets!

Choose someone who:

▶ Will not be put into an awkward position or harmed by learning your secret.

▶ You trust to hold this information as private while keeping you in their highest regard.

▶ Will not try to fix or save you but instead will listen objectively and compassionately.

▶ May have wisdom they can share with you.

▶ You trust.

▶ Your intuition is leading you toward.

▶ You have no attraction or sexual charge with. It is especially important not to tempt yourself with physical or emotional comfort from this person. It will distract you from the work and possibly end with more secrets.

Who can you share your secret with?

As you say goodbye to your secret for good,

and give it to faith, pick one of the following ways to let it go symbolically.

- Burn or bury your secret-breaking template.

- Get a rock or a stone and throw it into a body of water to symbolize washing away the secret.

- Write a letter to the false self, thanking her for all that she's done for you and for the secret itself. Let her know that your true self will now be leading.

- Put the secret in your God box (it can be a shoebox or anything else that might work for you) and shut the lid on it.

- Talk to your God about your secret and get a spiritual viewpoint.

Dirty Little Deep Dives

This is the last time your secret will ever be a secret.

You are a warrior.

Get into action and tell your secret.

Your true self is taking ownership of your life and that's a good thing.

Stage EIGHT

STOP CREATING SECRETS

Get ready because you are going to stand a little taller,

dream a little bigger, and love a little deeper.

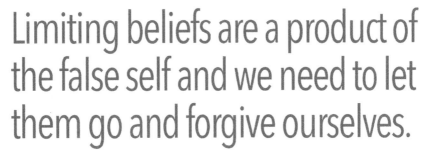

Limiting beliefs are a product of the false self and we need to let them go and forgive ourselves.

At their core, limiting beliefs are any beliefs that you hold about yourself or the world that keep you stuck. They can extend to beliefs about groups of people, society, and individuality. Let's find yours.

Identify and write down a limiting belief that you have about yourself that holds you back.

Challenge the belief by asking yourself: is it 100 percent true?

If you can't think of an instance in your own life where it isn't true, think about other people you know or have heard of and look for places where it might not be true. Write down your findings.

Since it's not 100 percent true, what could you believe instead?

If you believed that, what action would you take?

What else? What else? Give three answers to drop from your head, to your mouth, to your heart. (Answer this three different times.)

What else? What else? Give three answers to drop from your head, to your mouth, to your heart. (Answer this three different times)

If you took that new action,
what might happen?

If it feels hard, unlikely, or uncomfortable to take this step, think about another time in your life when you did something that you didn't think you could do, but you did it anyway? ————————

What did you learn from that experience that you can apply to this?

Write a letter to your false self thanking her for all that she's done to protect you,

the secrets she held close to keep you safe, and the actions she's taken to help you thrive. Let her know that your true self can take care of her now and that her faulty wiring, limiting beliefs and secret-keeping are no longer needed. Grant her forgiveness for what she did and didn't know. Assure her that you are committed to stepping into a secret-free life full of purpose.

Use these next few pages to write your letter, draw a picture, or do whatever is needed to grant forgiveness.

You can't live with unforgiveness and choose freedom. The resentments will always pull you back into the limiting beliefs of the false self.

Did I keep or create any secrets today (actions or stories that support my critical narrator and false identity)? Yes/No and explore.

If so, what root or tripwire feeling, faulty
wiring, or limiting belief was at play?

Dirty Little
Deep Dives

Be gentle with your
false self and thank her,
truly, deepy and
completely for all that
she's done for you so
that you can make
room for your true self.

Forgiveness is the cornerstone
to letting go of the false self.

It's time for you to put on your
red heels and shatter the
limiting beliefs of your glass
ceiling.

Watch out for secret-keeping
landmines by doing a daily
secret-keeping check-in.

Stage NINE

DEATH OF THE OLD YOU

It's time to say goodbye to say hello.

STAGE NINE
DEATH OF THE OLD YOU
PART 1: KNOW YOUR TRIGGERS

It's important for you to know what trips you up so that when the Old You is activated, you can take contrary action. Think of your secret and use the work you have already done in Stages One through Eight to crystalize the following:

What is your faulty wiring?

(reference Stage Two, Part One)

What is your tripwire emotion?

(reference Stage Two, Part Two)

What is your root feeling?

(reference Stage Three, Part One)

What is another way to get your root feeling met?

Hint, it is never by acting in your Old Self.

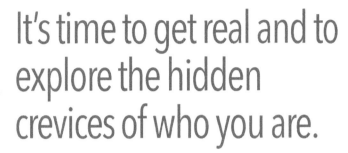

It's time to get real and to explore the hidden crevices of who you are.

Answer the following questions as honestly as possible. They range in depth and are meant to help you to become curious about who you are. Allow yourself to go with your gut when you answer. Give yourself time to thoroughly answer the questions. Self-discovery is a gift and shouldn't be rushed.

What comes naturally to you?

What do people come to you for?

What's your superpower (something that you do better than most people)?

What do you like the most about yourself?

What organizations/ causes
do you care about?

Where do you feel
called to give back?

What talents do you have?

What are your gifts?

What people, places, and situations do you feel the most energized from?

What hidden dream or desire do you keep coming back to even if you haven't taken action on it?

_____

What inklings do you have about what you are here to do?

Your New You is 100 percent, authentically you, owns her power, knows what she likes and doesn't like, and is interested in self-discovery. As you get to know the New You, take an honest look at your hidden thoughts. It's important to spell these out so that they don't become secrets.

What do you feel is off-putting or obnoxious about you?

What are your most unpopular thoughts/beliefs?

What opinions do you keep to yourself?

DEATH OF THE OLD YOU
PART 3: DEFINE YOUR HIGHEST VALUES

Tools like step-by-step guides, worksheets, and personality tests are available online and in many coaching books to determine your personal values. My favorite way to help people find their values takes a different approach and should help you to get to the heart of what you value quickly.

Don't overthink it. Feel it.

Write down a list of pet peeves.

Flip your list to what you value.

THREE TIPS TO **NOT CREATE NEW VALUE SECRETS:**

Do a body check. If you've had an interaction and feel sick to your stomach, tense, nervous, or agitated, you are probably blurring your values and are on the verge of creating a secret that will go against them. Use your body for clues to see if you are out of alignment.

Post your values where you can see them. When you don't know what to do, ask yourself, what is my highest value? Take action on that and remind yourself of what your life was like when you were collecting secrets.

Your values are a way of life. Be willing to walk away from people and situations that might pull you into the Old You.

DEATH OF THE OLD YOU
PART 4: CREATE YOUR "I WON'T" LIST

List your open loops.

They might be business deals you toy with, men you think about dating, exes you fantasize about getting back together with, tasks that you feel obligated to do, projects that are shiny, and so on.

List your open loops.

Circle any that are a full-body, hell yes that you are certain the New You wants to take action on.

Based on the values of the New You, create an I Won't list
from the open loops of anything that is not a hell yes—therefore, closing the loop. These can be things like going back to school to get a master's degree, volunteering, cleaning underneath your bed, networking with people from high school, or partnering with that person who has an interesting idea that you have very little desire to do.

Closing loops has power, keeps you in alignment with the New You, and ushers out the Old You and her critical narrator.

Don't be shy. Let's flaunt what you've got.
The key to this exercise is to start noticing your impact.

What are the positive things that people say about you?

Start keeping an ongoing list so that you can see how you show up in the world.

Write down the ways that you have helped others and created a positive impact.

Read it daily.
End it with,
"who you are
makes a difference."

Dirty Little Deep Dives

Commit 100 percent to the new you and say goodbye to the old you.

Contrary action is your go-to tool.

You have purpose, power and potential.

Who you are makes a difference.

CREATING YOUR
RIPPLE EFFECT

Step into your purpose and bigger living.

It's so easy to go into auto-pilot, check-out, multi-task and go fast.

For the next week, you are going to intentionally pay attention to the ripple you create and notice how others respond.

Take note of your interactions with everyone you encounter, from the mailman, the repairman, the grocer, your cleaning lady, your kids, friends, parents, husband, co-workers, and neighbors. How do you behave with them? What response do you get in return?

Pick a day and be intentional about saying hello to everyone you encounter with a smile on your face. Thoughtfully send them good feelings as you interact or pass by them. Make eye contact wherever possible. Note your ripple.

In a separate journal, notice your energy levels and write down the difference in your interactions when your energy level was high versus low.

Pay attention to your low or agitated energy and notice the difference in how others respond to you and the feeling left in the room versus when your energy is fueled with positivity.

What is your go-to energy feeling? Knowing what feeling you are predisposed to is a key to shifting your energy to create a different ripple.

Example: dread, excitement, optimism, love, agitation, anxiety.

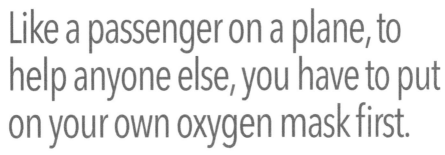

Like a passenger on a plane, to help anyone else, you have to put on your own oxygen mask first.

Answer the following questions to help you
define how you will get your oxygen.

What kind of emotional and mental support do you need on an ongoing basis so that you don't slide backward and create more secrets?

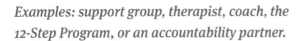

*Examples: support group, therapist, coach, the
12-Step Program, or an accountability partner.*

What do you do for physical fitness and how often?

What daily practice will help you to start your day on solid footing?

How can you connect to
Your God more often?

What professionals do you
need to see for self-care?

*Examples: doctor for a
checkup, mammogram,
dentist, chiropractor,
acupuncturist, and so on.*

What fills your tank that feels indulgent?

Examples: massage, nails, girls' trips, workshops.

What do you do for fun?

_____

What do you do for self-development?

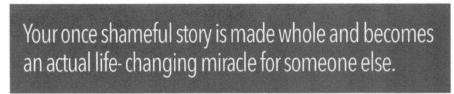
Your once shameful story is made whole and becomes an actual life- changing miracle for someone else.

Close your eyes and imagine two years into the future.

Where do you live?

What risk did you take to make your life of an intention a life of commitment?

What dream are you living?

Are you in a community of action?

Who do you serve?

What makes you the most proud?

Are you feeling loved
by those around you?

Who is your biggest support?

What feelings do you experience most often?

What ripple are you creating?

___

Reflect on your answers. What do you need to do in order future into the present?

What intention do you need to create
and partner with committed action?

*Dirty Little
Deep Dives*

Your secret is
a lifesaving gift to
you and to others.
It's the miracle
underneath.

Self-care is the cornerstone
to living as the new you.

Every intention needs
commitment and action.

Sharing your secret is a
beacon of hope that will
free another woman.

Our intentions built on commitment become the actions that we take that create our ripple effect.

As you move forward, always keep this question in mind, **"Will my New You be grateful for the decisions I'm making today, or will these decisions lead to more secret-keeping?"** The rewards of this new way of living have only just begun. It's time to open your hands and your heart and let that new way of being seep through you from the top of your head to the tip of your toes, knowing that you are now partnered with your New You and that your secret was always the miracle underneath!

Much love, Gretchen